Folens

AGE 8–9

Accessing...

SCIENCE 4

Acknowledgements

Action Plus/Glyn Kirk: 39, 40
Alamy/John T Fowler: 9 (bottom)
Alamy/Leslie Garland Picture Library: 16 (top right)
Alamy/Maximilian Weinzierl: 29 (top right)
Britain on View: 36 (right)
Bryn Williams/Crash.net: 38 (right)
Christine Moorcroft: 14 (bl); 14 (br); 15 (bl); 15 (c); 21 (tl); 22 (tl); 29 (l); 32 (tr); 37 (br); 38 (l); 47; 48
CORBIS/Bettman: 4; /The Purcell Team: 5 (l); /Enzo & PaoloRagazzini: 6 (b); /Brandon D. Cole: 9 (t); /ER Productions: 11; /Lester V. Bergman: 12; /Chris Hellier: 13 (bl); /Mark A. Johnson: 13 (br); /Steve Austin; Papillo: 14 (tl); /Nick Hawkes; Ecoscene: 14 (tr); /Arthur Morris: 15 (tl); /Tom Brakefield: 15 (tr); /Tony Hamblin; Frank Lane Picture Agency: 16 (tl); /Niall Benvie: 16 (b); /Michael Gore; Frank Lane Picture Agency: 17; /Brian Vikander: 18; /Niall Benvie: 21; /Galen Rowell: 22 (bl); /Wolfgang Kaehler: 22 (c); /Jim Sugar Photography: 24 (l); /Photowood Inc: 24 (tr); /Layne Kennedy: 24 (br); /Jeffrey L Rotman: 26 (l); /Pierre Schwartz: 29 (br); /Joseph Sohm: 30 (l); /Fukuhara: 30 (tr); /Charles Gold: 30 (br); /Jeffrey L. Rotman: 32 (tl); /Charles O'Rear: 33 (t); /Macduff Everton: 33 (b); /Pete Stone: 35 (l); /Dimitri Iundt: 35 (r); /Kevin R. Morris: 37 (tl); /Dennis Marsico: 37 (tr); /Peter Russell; The Military Picture Library: 41; /Kevin R. Morris: 42
DIY Photo Library: 28
FLPA/David Hosking: 15 (bottom right)
Horton Levi Ltd: 27 (top)
Martin Sookias: 26 (right)
National Trust/Nick Meers: 36 (left)
NHPA/George Bernard: 6 (top)
NHPA/Michael Leach: 5 (right)
Pentland Outdoor Division/Berghaus: 25 (socks courtesy of Brasher outdoor footwear)
Powerstock/Superstock: 23 (bottom)
Rebecca Thompson: 31; 32 (bottom left); 32 (bottom right); 37 (bottom left); 44
Science Photo Library: 8
Science Photo Library/Alfred Pasieka: 13 (top left)
Science Photo Library/Sheila Terry: 10
Science Photo Library/Tony McConnell: 27 (bottom)
Wellcome Photo Library/Sarah-Jane Smith: 7
Whirlpool (UK) Ltd 22 (top right and bottom right); 23 (top)

United Kingdom: Folens Publishers, Apex Business Centre, Boscombe Road, Dunstable, LU5 4RL.
Email: folens@folens.com

Ireland: Folens Publishers, Greenhills Road, Tallaght, Dublin 24.
Email: info@folens.ie

Poland: JUKA, ul. Renesansowa 38, Warsaw 01-905.

Editor: Jennifer Steele
Layout artist: Patricia Hollingsworth
Illustrations: Alan Baker: 19, 23 (top); Steve Caldwell (Allied Artists): 20, 22, 23 (bottom), 24, 34, 43, 45, 46
Cover design: Martin Cross
Cover image: CORBIS/Jim Sugar

First published 2005 by Folens Limited.

British Library Cataloguing in Publication Data. A catalogue record for this publication is available from the British Library.

ISBN 1 84303 549 9

Contents

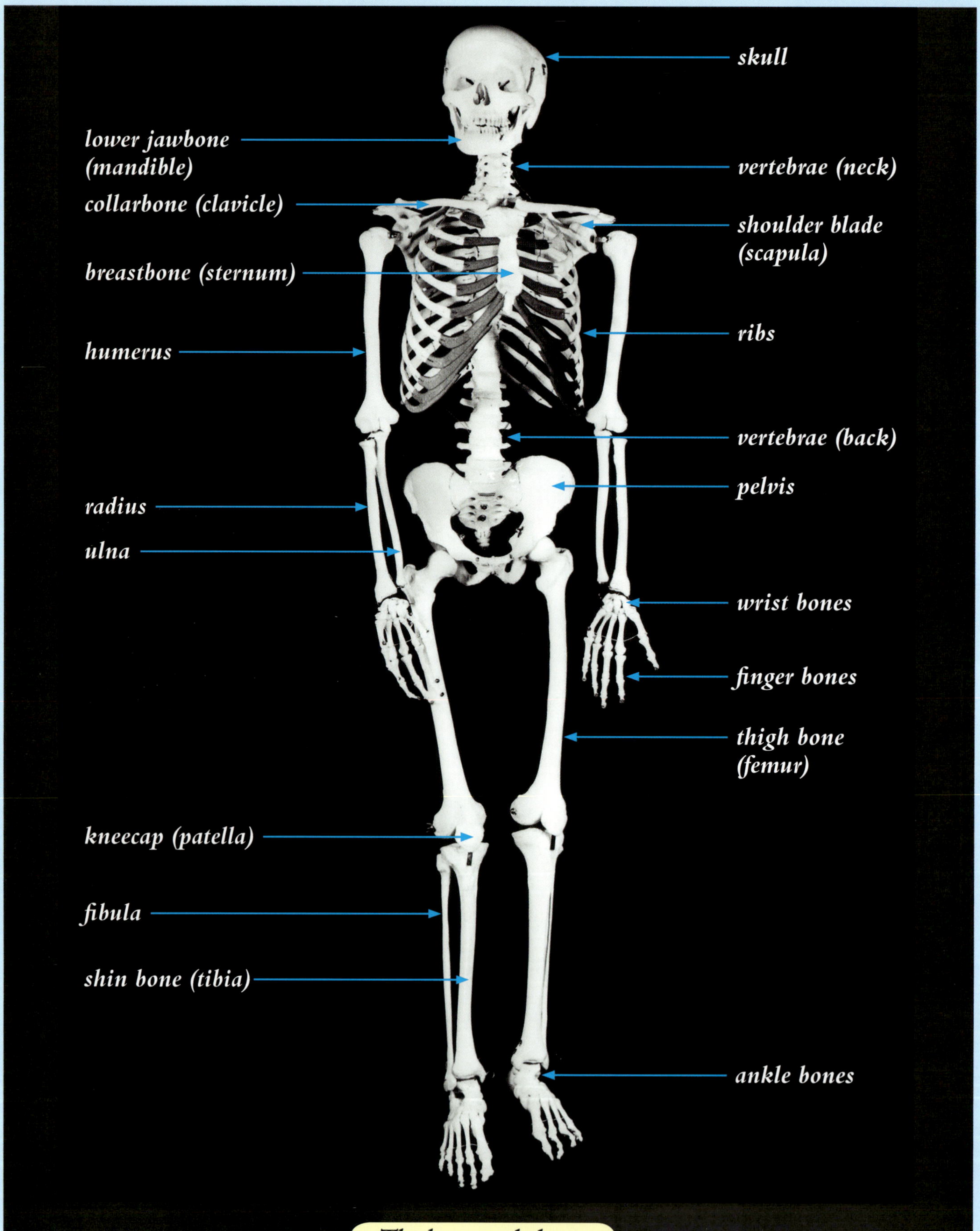

The human skeleton

Animal skeletons (1)

A snake

An owl

Animal skeletons (2)

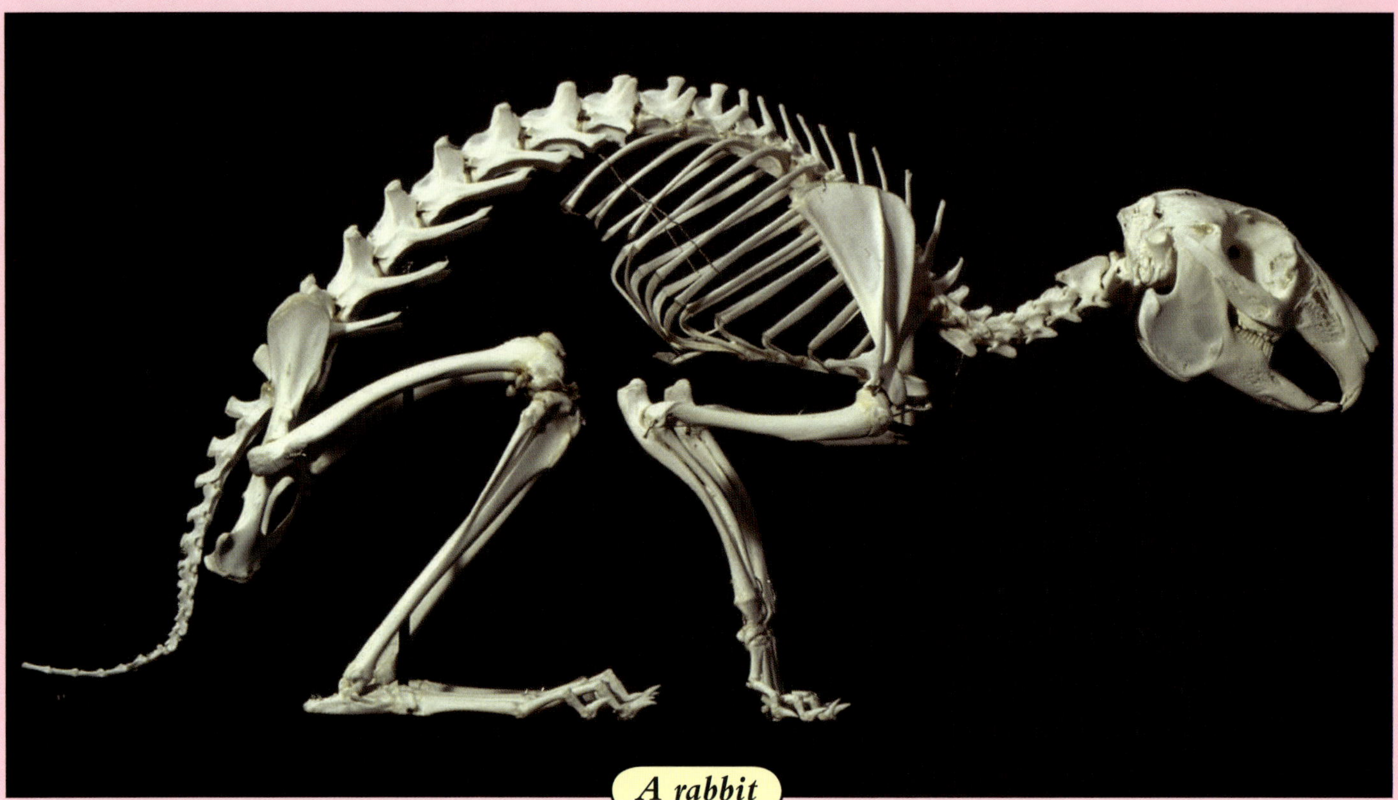

A rabbit

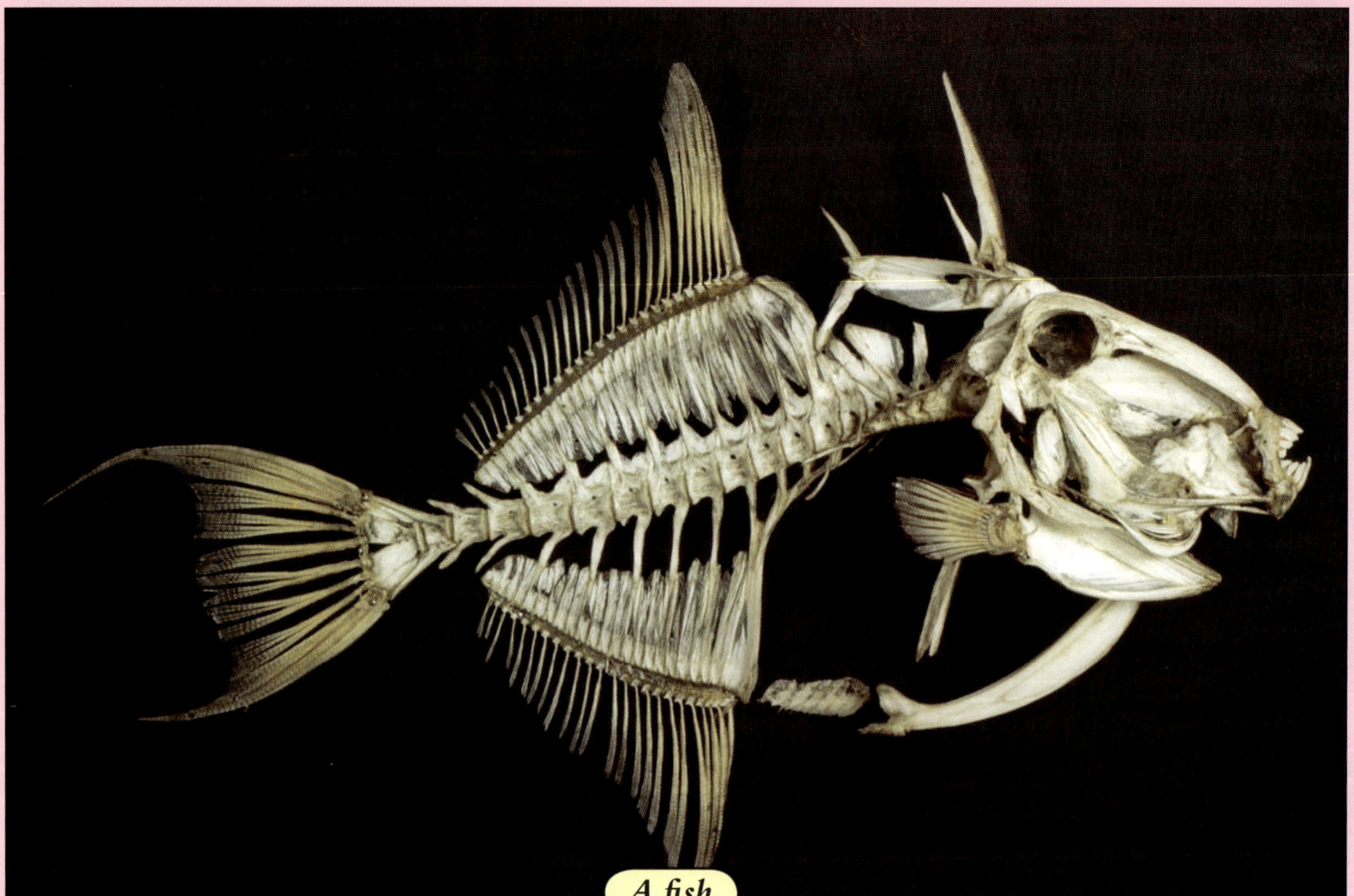

A fish

Our growing skull

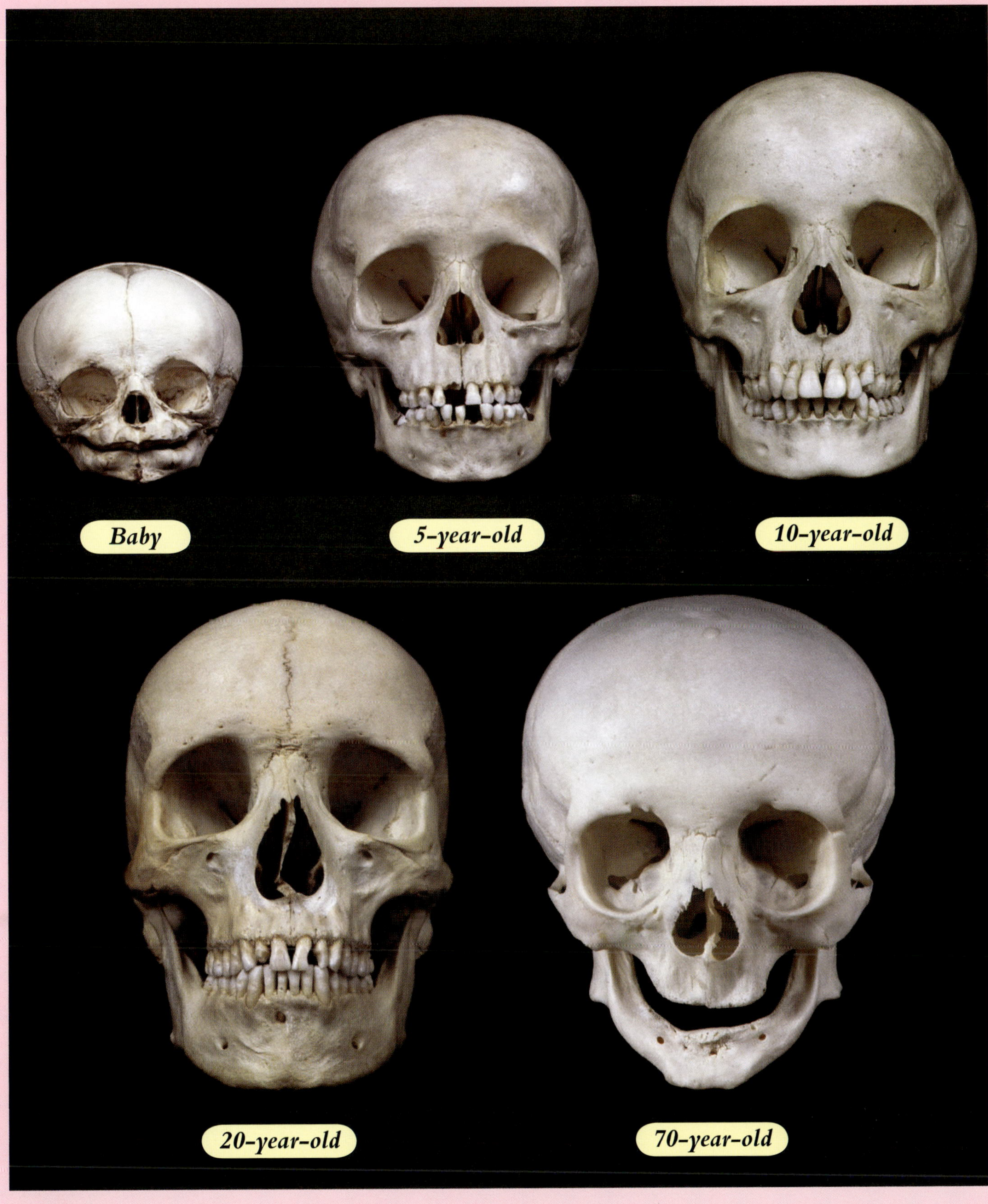

Our growing hands

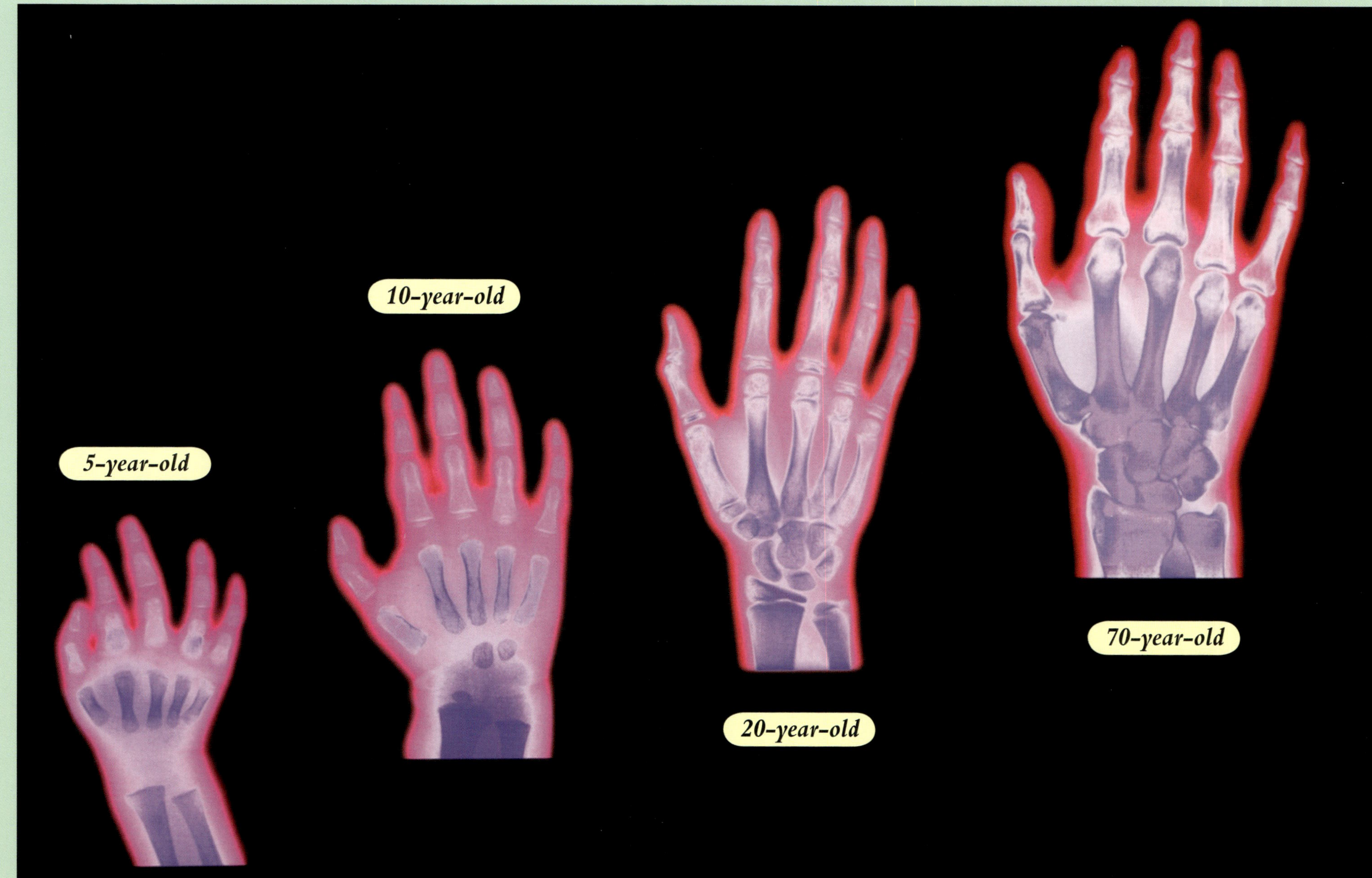

Animals without backbones

A jellyfish

An earthworm

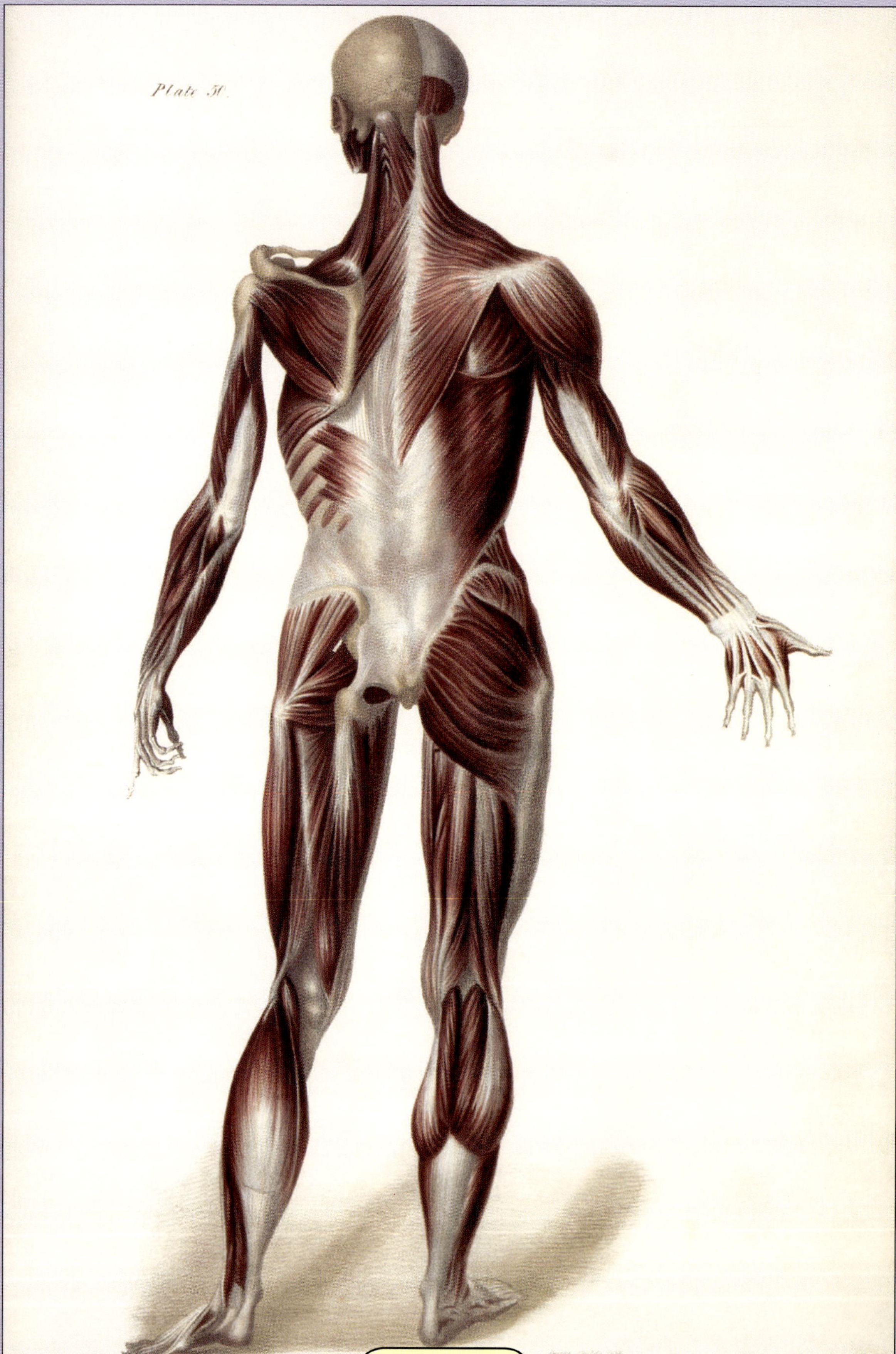

Muscles

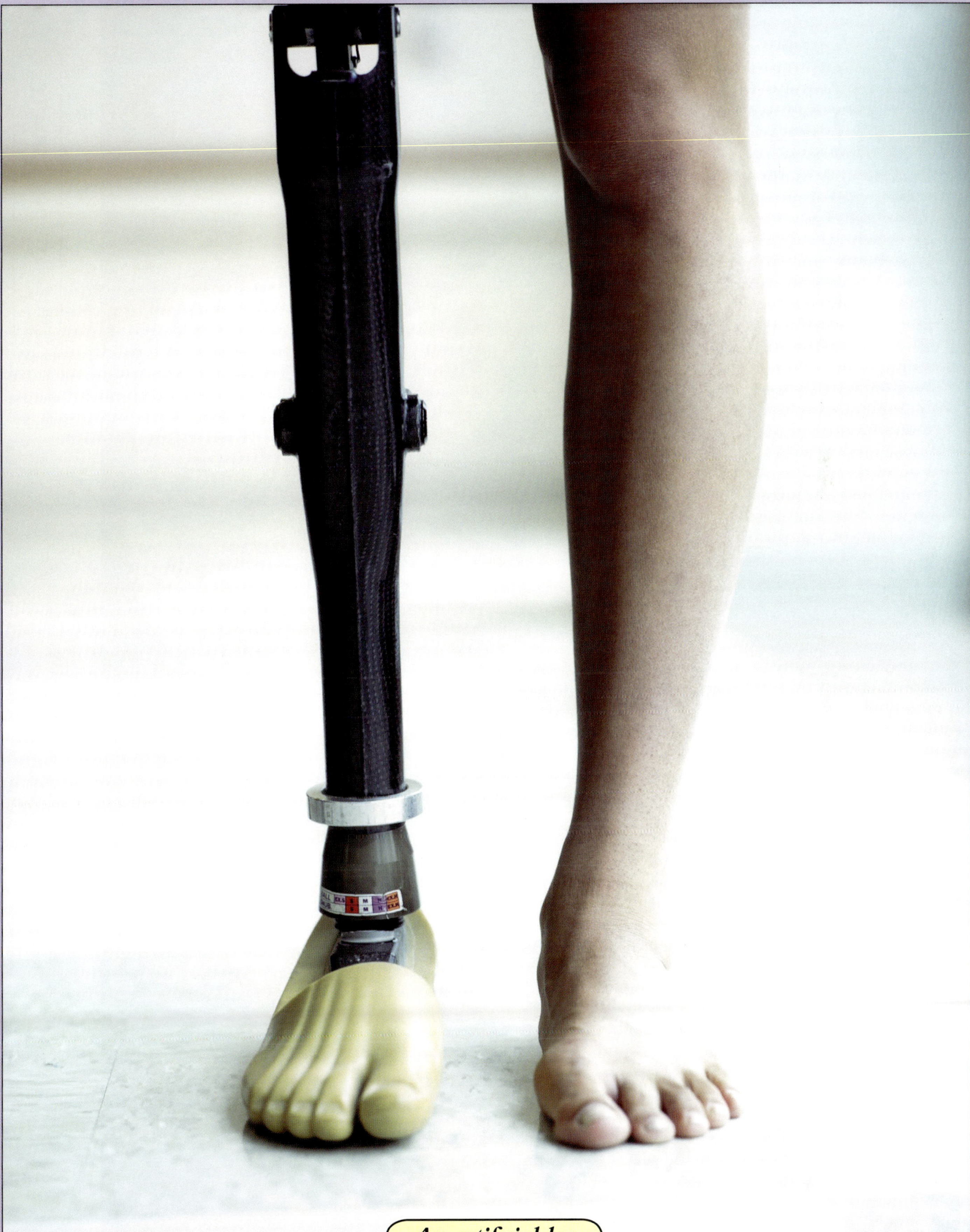

An artificial leg

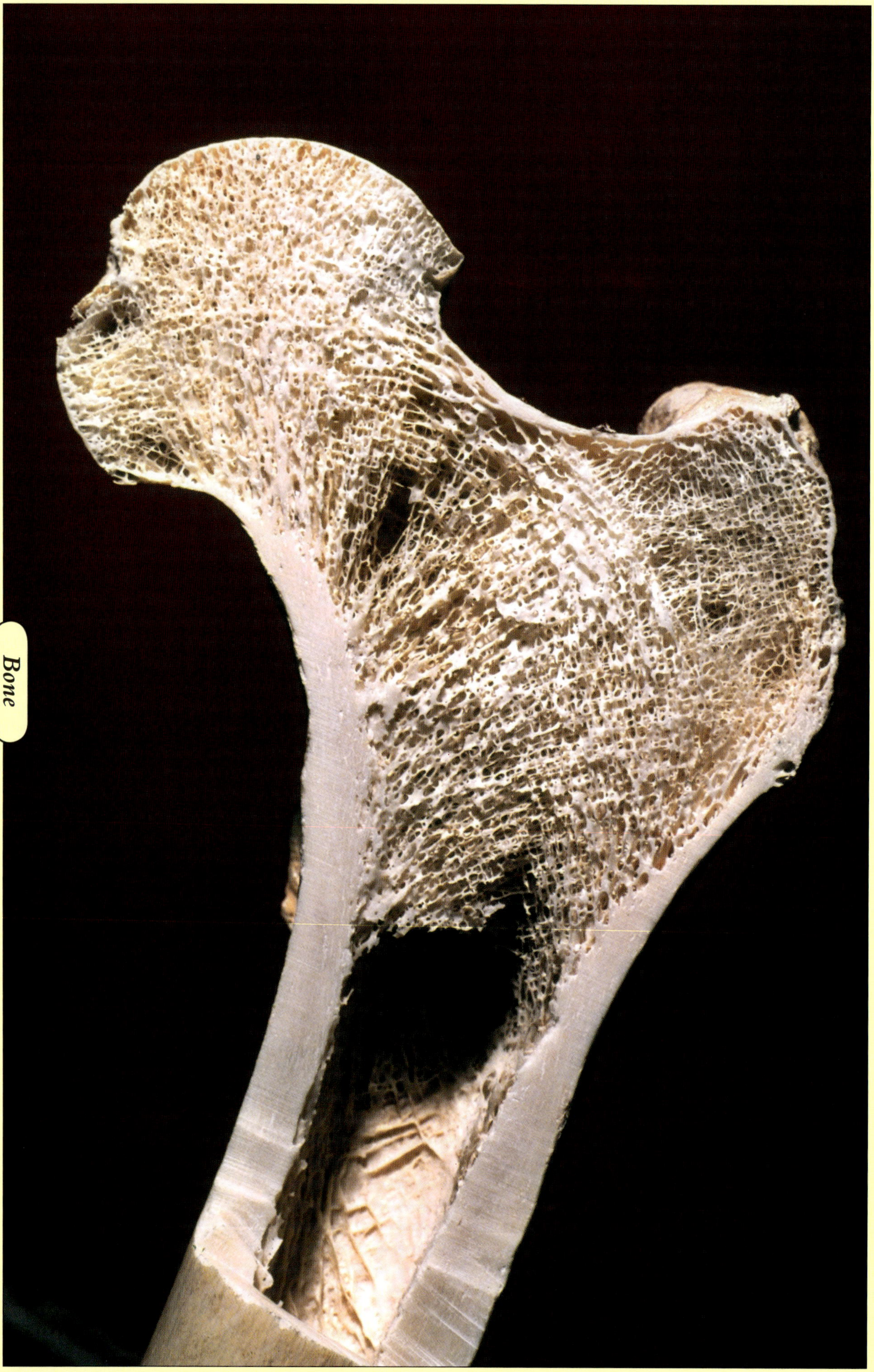

Animals and animal-like organisms

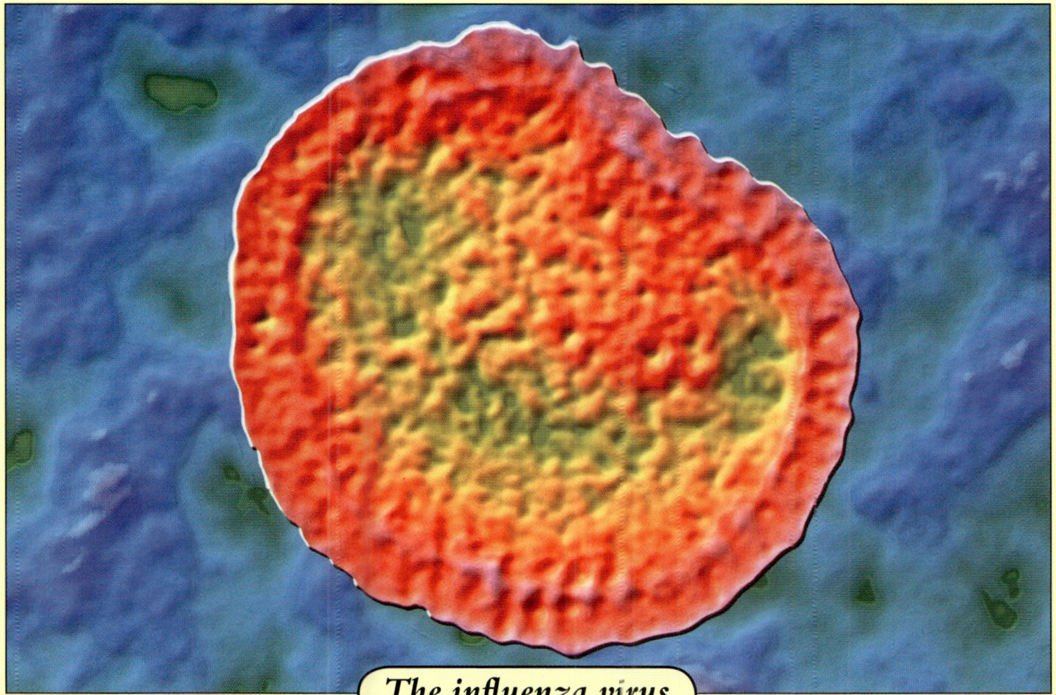

The influenza virus

A scorpion

A peacock

Plants and plant-like organisms

An ash tree

Algae

Mushrooms

A rose

A moorland habitat

A sand dune habitat

A skylark

Sand dunes

Sea rocket

The Arctic fox

The dromedary

City birds

Starling – 21.5cm
Pigeon – 41cm
House Sparrow – 14.5cm
Magpie – 46cm
House Martin – 12.5cm
Swallow – 19cm
Swift – 16.5cm

Food chains

Endangered animals

A red squirrel

Low temperatures

High temperatures (1)

Air inside an oven

Molten iron

High temperatures (2)

A volcano

The Sahara Desert

A hot spring

Polartec® trousers

Polyester T-shirt

Merino wool and Meraklon® fibre sock

Polartec® gloves

Polartec® fleece

Polartec® hat

Hot and cold food containers

Fish for delivery

Hot food being delivered to a school

Thermal images

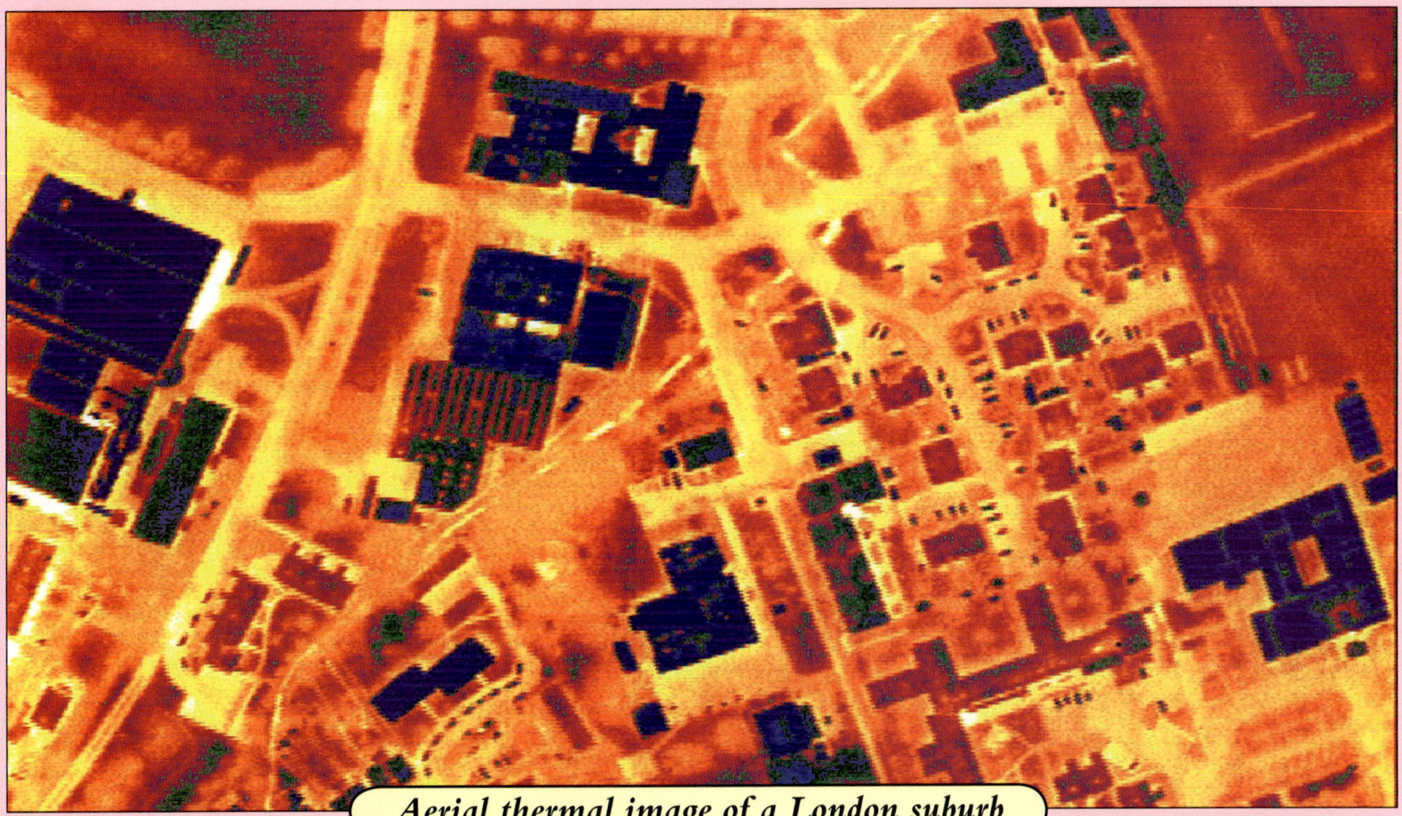

Aerial thermal image of a London suburb

Thermal image of houses

Keeping a house warm

Loft insulation

Solids

Concrete

Stones

Sand

Liquids

Water

Milk

Syrup

Volume

1 litre
2.5 litres
2 litres
1.5 litres
500ml
5 litres
HIGHLAND
SPRING
volvic
Natural Mineral Water
Mr Muscle
ANTI-BACTERIAL ACTION
Tropicana
PURE PREMIUM
ORIGINAL
Indulge yourself for free
Ribena
NEW COVENT GARDEN FOOD Co
Seasonal Soups
EXTRA VIRGIN
125ml
1 litre
1 litre
500ml
500ml

Separators

A net

A coffee filter

A vegetable strainer

A riddle

Melting points

Molten gold (melting point 1065°C)

Molten glass (melting point varies between 500–1650°C)

Kitchen solutions

Pushes and pulls

Tug-of-war

Weightlifting

Isaac Newton

Woolsthorpe Manor, Woolsthorpe-by-Colsterworth, nr Grantham, Lincolnshire

Statue of Isaac Newton in Grantham, Lincolnshire

Surfaces

Gravel

Marble

Tarmac

Concrete

Tyres

Tractor tyres

Racing car tyres

Diving

A rowing boat

A jet

A parachute

Faulty circuits

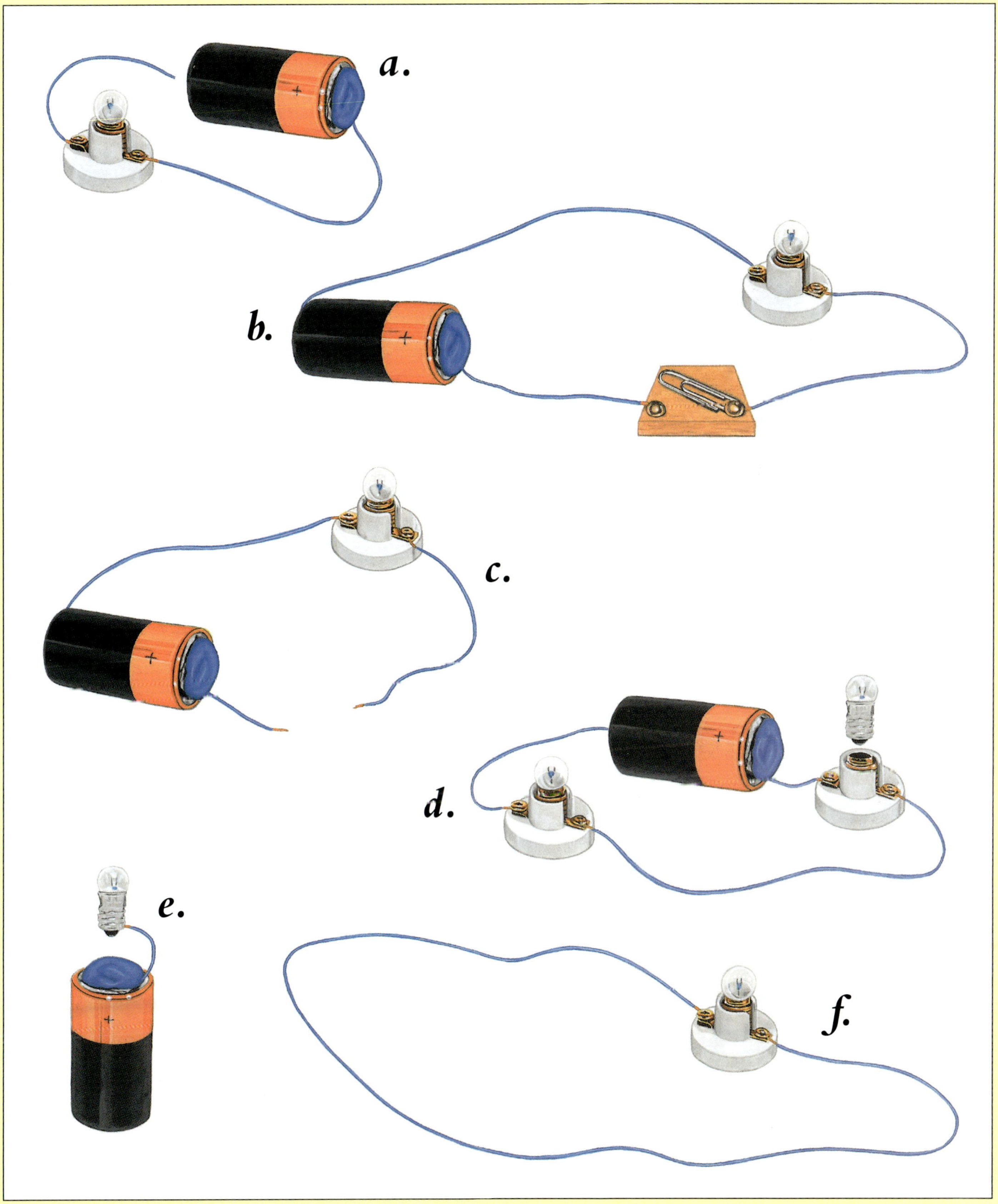

A light bulb

Conductors and insulators

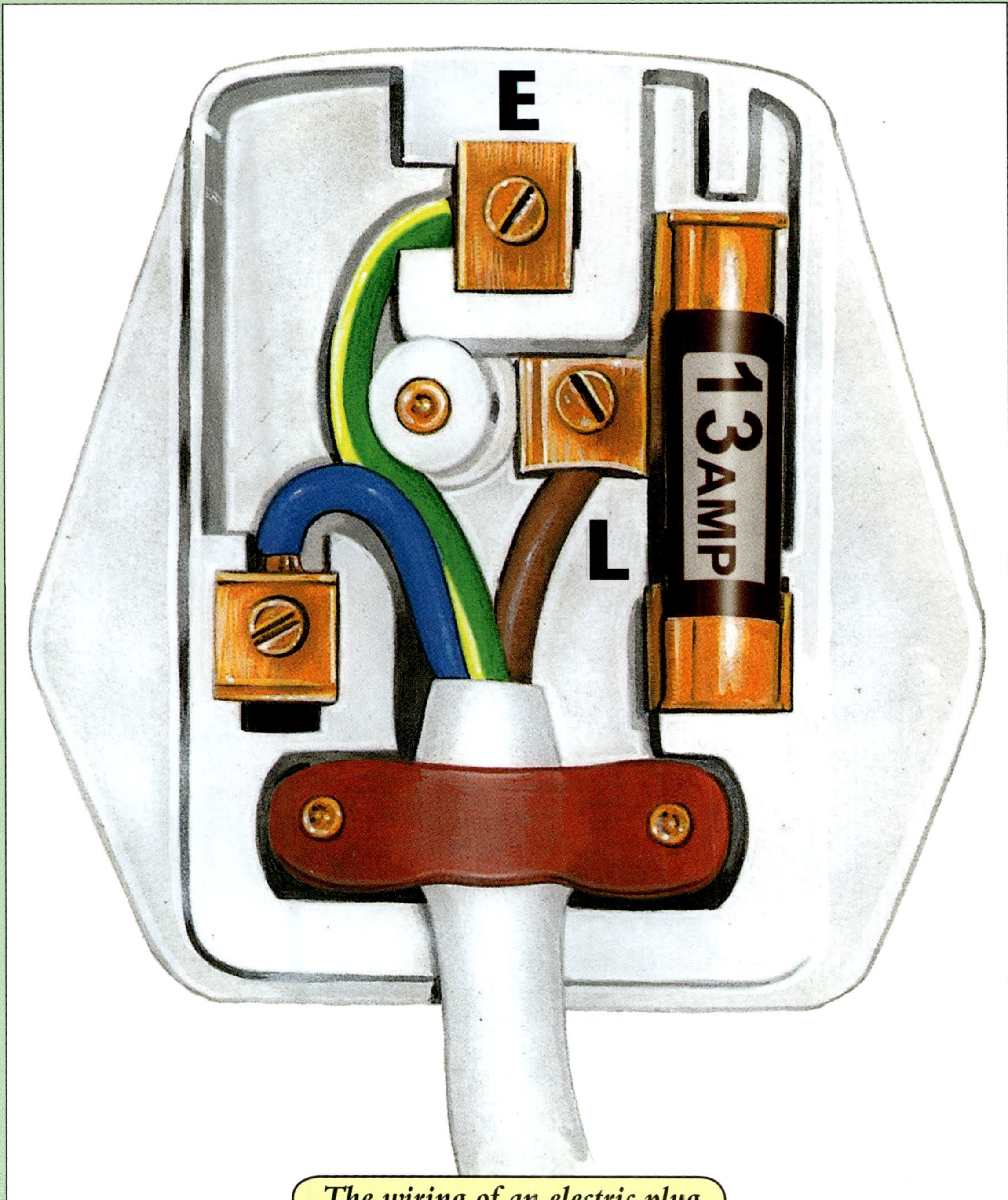

The wiring of an electric plug

An electric socket

Crazy circuits

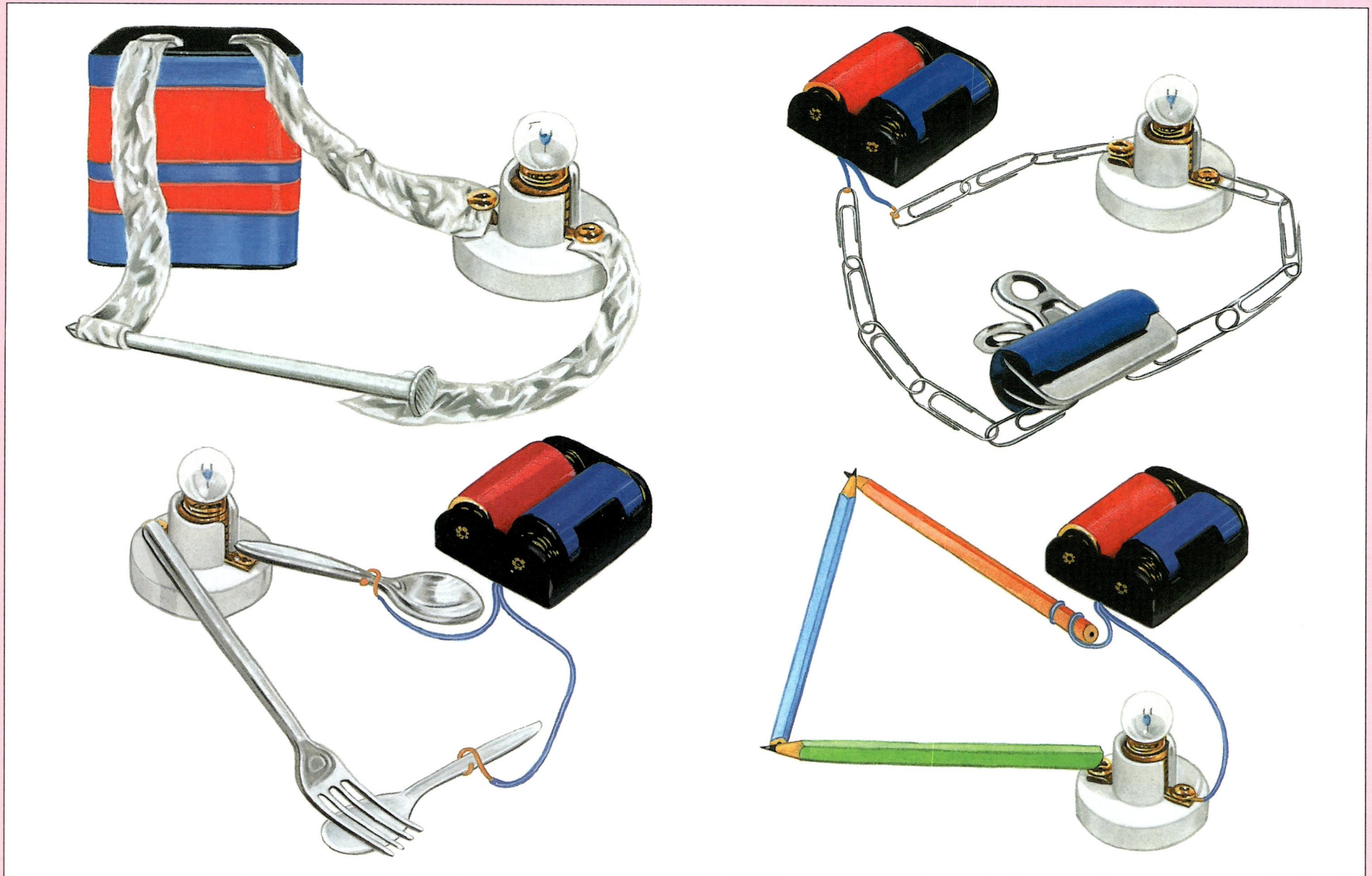

Torches and their batteries

A dolls' house with lights